I, The Golden Star

A MAGICAL STORY OF TRANSFORMATION
BASED ON TRUE EVENTS

Illustrated by Stephanie Chinn

ISBN: 978-1-952779-38-1
Library of Congress Control Number: 2020912700

FIG
FACTOR
MEDIA

Dedication:

To Ogunbiyi, my mentor, partner and spiritual guide. He who always pushed me to write and do my best. Love and light wherever you are.

Acknowledgments:

I want to thank the Supreme Soul for giving me inner seeing. Iyaniwura-Oshun for tasting your sweet waters and shedding light upon me. My daughters for giving me inspiration, insight and igniting my curiosity. My family, my mom, abuelita, brother and sister that helped me through this creative process and never gave up on me. My spiritual family, Shivbaba, Krutimata, Poornima and the Elebuibon family. Omi Eleti Elegua for believing in this story, helping me since day one and calling it like it was. Stephanie Chin, gifted artist, you made this book more magical. Jacqueline Camacho-Ruiz for coming to my rescue, helped me through this exceptional project and made this book a physical manifestation. I can't thank you enough. All of you are dear to my heart. Thank you for helping me in this lifetime.

*T*he **Oshun River**. A mystical place where the seen and unseen walk together nestled in the rainforest of West Africa in a town called Oshogbo, Nigeria. For many people, this river is sacred and has supernatural healing powers. Oshun represents the feminine power and every year in August there is a festival dedicated to Oshun the river Deity-divinity.

5

In a place where the seen and unseen walk together lived a young man by the name of Ogunbiyi, he was also known as El Caballero de Ifa. The final three letters of his second name are deeply revered in the Yoruba culture. "Ifa" symbolizes a spiritual center, in which every being possesses a destiny. Ifa is regarded as the witness of all destinies.

Ogunbiyi was full of light, his world was a place where the sun shines year-round and the waters are as sweet as a mother's kiss. With his charismatic personality, a smile as wide as the crescent moon, dark almond shape eyes and his internal essence as bright as the sun, he touched many hearts and turned them into gold.

7

But even his goodness could not readily strike the evil that grew like weeds among the world's farthest corners, an evilness that had slowly grown over time. Ogunbiyi thought about the dangers ahead as he walked along the Oshun River.

The most astonishing part was that Ogunbiyi lived in a place where he was able to see two worlds and was able to mediate in both worlds. One world was obvious; it was made of flesh and bone. The other world existed only by sensing life through vibration. Only a few understood this world because it was not visually seen but rather, could be felt.

Ogunbiyi was always curious and grateful to be able to walk on earth. He was known to have a special relationship with Oshun the river Goddess. Every day he would offer special Kola nuts to Oshun. He would take some of the small nuts in his hands, crack them open and whisper on the kola nuts. After his petitions to Oshun, he would leave the kola nuts by the riverbank and clear his mind by staying in remembrance of his soul while being on earth. In those moments, he tried to create a wider chasm between the people and place he loved and the evil ones that existed in the monolithic world, a world of the unfortunates.

This other world was where a woman by the name of Tola lived. She lived where the majority of humans lived who were able to see only one world, the world made of flesh and bones.

Tola was influenced by a society where people saw the superficial parts of themselves and others. As the years passed, an emptiness fell in the hearts of humans and the beginning of discontent allowed to enter their hearts. There was no unity. Mental and physical sickness started to rise. Nature became unbalanced by the negative vibrations that were being produced by humans. This world operated in a superficial level where material things became more important than the purity of the heart.

*T*ola was a sensitive person. This meant that she could feel what others could feel and pick up on thoughts and energy of others. Her mind could sense many things that others could not see or sense. This was a gift from the creator that Tola herself did not recognize. She would question herself in the mirror and would say:

13

Every day was a struggle with her own persona, picking up on others vibrations and not knowing what to do with that energy. She filled her head with sorrowful thoughts and a heavy blanket of distress covered her smallest joy. She felt lost in the universe, looking and focusing only on the superficial parts of herself and others.

Although her eyes become covered with the superficial aspect of herself, deep inside her heart she knew there was more than just the superficial level. She just couldn't figure out the missing piece of her life and her true purpose on earth.

Tola had heard and read stories of Oshun, the river goddess. She was intrigued with Oshun's mysterious powers. She admired all the stories of courage, love, understanding and bliss. Yet she understood the destruction of Oshun in order to bring balance to the lives of people and the world.

When the moon sat high in the sky, Tola had a dream about a beautiful radiant star at the Oshun River. As she tried to reach for the star, the silhouette of a young man appeared next to her looking straight at her. With out a single word, he stretched his arms towards her and granted her a radiant gold star. Her eyes opened, then closed again. She realized that she had been dreaming. The dream felt so real, that for a brief moment she felt the young man's presence next to her. She felt the need to go to the Oshun River. Gravity begged her to find the truth about her true self; it pulled her towards a light she could not see, but feel.

"I am determined to find something that I am missing but can't understand it yet. There is something that is pulling me towards my destiny and I feel the need to go and find what I am truly missing. I know for a fact that life is more than what we see with our two eyes I can sense it."

ola journeyed across the turbulent waters of the sea until she finally arrived in Nigeria. There were people left and right, like colonies of ants. People walking everywhere. Tola was looking left and right not knowing where to go. Suddenly, an old crone with a limping leg and earthy colors appeared from the crowd of people. She approached Tola and spoke to her.

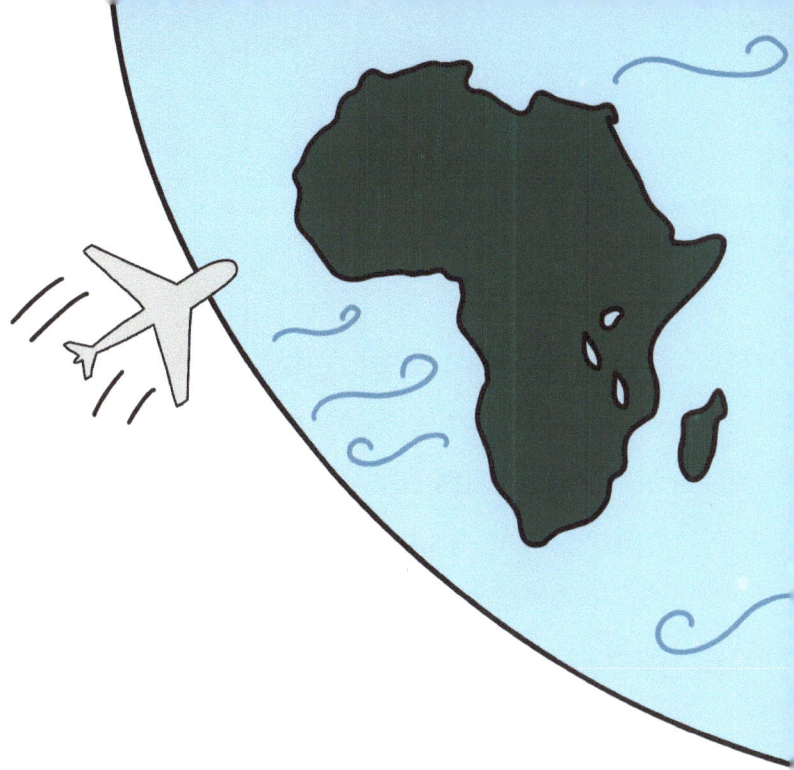

"Come with me child. I know you came from far to find your purpose of life. Oshun will guide you by helping you find your true essence."

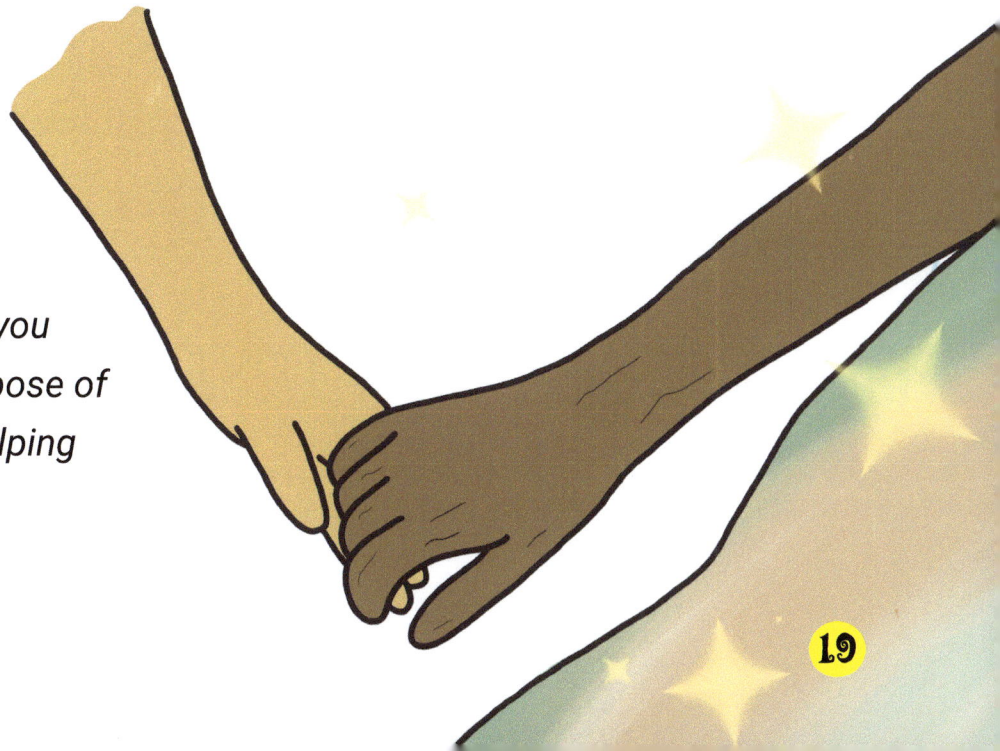

Tola felt the pureness of the old woman's heart and decided to go with her. They walked many hours. Tola felt tired and she could barely walk. The hot sun was at its shiniest and the perspiration was sliding down her skin. With her feet feeling as heavy as a rock she turned around to talk to the old crone but as soon as she turned her head, the old crone said, *"The earth heals and transforms, just like you, me and all of us."* The spirit of the woman with all her earthy colors faded, leaving behind the scent of fresh earth, a fragrance that hung in the air.

Tola was enlightened as she walked faster and the fresh earth smell became deeper. She started smelling the pure scent of untouched trees and flowers, the sweet sound and smell of fresh water and the healing waters of the Oshun River. She started walking with a much faster pace towards the riverbank. She could feel her heart bursting with joy and tears cascading down her face. But she was also experiencing sadness.

21

As Ogunbiyi walked along the Oshun River's edge, he saw Tola's tears. He felt the woman's distress and quickly approached her and asked, "What's the matter? Why are you crying?" Tola, who was kneeling by the riverbank turned and looked up and saw a young, tall man. She lifted her arm and placed her hand on the side of her forehead like an open canopy. A bright light was bothering her eyes.

   She noticed that he was the young man from her dream. This time his eyes were big and shinny like the radiant sky in midday. They had a special shimmer that was pouring out from them. The woman, wiping her tears from her cheeks replied.

"My name is Tola and I am on a mission to find my true purpose. I am walking without thinking and my mind is like a wild horse; it never stops running!"

I see myself with loathing because the expectations that I have in order to fit in are much greater. I just don't know how I can fit in a world of superficial expectations. People only see themselves and others for what they have on the outside but they don't go deeper and see what really is important.

Ogunbiyi was able to sense Tola's uncertainty and sadness and said to her, *"You feel lost because you forgot who you truly are."*

Tola, with her eyes still wet, muttered *"What are you talking about?" "Don't you see I am a woman?"*

With a smile as white as the full moon, he sat next to her and gently spoke to her, *"You came to earth for a reason and you have been in this circle of life's ups and downs. Life is a precious gift. And yes, you are a woman! You have brown eyes, yes! You are made out of flesh and bone, yes! But that's not who you truly are. You can have dark or light skin color that is not your reality because your body is only a costume. You are more than what you see with your two eyes."*

Ogunbiyi continued to speak, *"The soul sheds bodies just as the body sheds clothes. When you sing, dance, write or perform any activity, your body parts are the ones doing the job. You tell your body what to do and it will do it. The body is a precious and delicate gift we need to take care like a newborn."*

draw
play
dance
create
flow

"Though you only see the body, your real self is a light and it is so bright that is called SOUL, your inner essence. A tiny light but with enormous power is situated in between your two eyebrows. Like the stars living in the sky, you are a living star on the planet earth. You just don't remember who you are because you only see your body, your eyes, hair, nose and ears through your five senses like the five elements on earth: earth, wind, fire, water, and sky."

*T*ola looked at Ogunbiyi with amazement because she had never heard that before. The lyrical voice of Ogunbiyi was a delight to her ears. There was something magical in the air, something that felt just right but also out of this physical realm.

Ogunbiyi remarked, *"Remember, you are far more than what you see and sense with your five senses. Just visualize you have a star in between your two eyebrows. This is where your shining star resides and in order to access that star, you need to be able to remember the SOUL at all times."*

"If you want to feel the star, you need to practice by remembering who you truly are. You are the star situated between your two eyebrows. Did you know that the star has all the treasures that make you feel good like peace, happiness, courage, understanding, freedom and most important love?" His poetic voice fell on the ears of Tola like a precious lotus flower.

"You received all of those gifts when you were born and all of those gifts are inside you, the star. When you are born, your star is so bright that everyone that sees you wants to hold you, hug you and kiss you. You are creative. You love without limits and you enjoy every moment. But the more you keep growing and start seeing only the body, the star loses a little bit of shine. Each year your star keeps diminishing. You become more afraid of things. You are worried about what others are going to say or if they are even going to like you, until one day your star drowns completely because of being body conscious. You lose track of your star and you start seeing yourself and others as a body. See, the star is like a battery. If you don't charge it by remembering it, you will not be able to feel the star anymore."

"When you are remembering your shining star, your thoughts become positive and peaceful and you are good to yourself and others. Your thoughts are very powerful because each thought has a vibration that releases either positive or negative vibrations into the atmosphere. Therefore, when you walk in two worlds, you are walking on earth seeing through your physical eyes and walking in the invisible world of the soul. You need to start connecting inside of you, remembering your light inside. You have to think; I am a special Soul and therefore, everything of mine should be special. By focusing your mind in yourself, the shining star, you are able to create pure thoughts and those thoughts have their own vibrations. Be conscious of your thoughts, words, and actions. Everything has a vibration that eventually has an effect on you, others and the world."

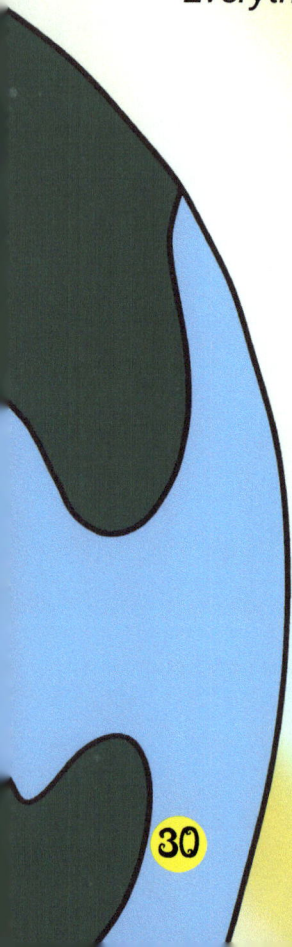

31

After listening to this, Tola turned around and stared at the Oshun River. Ogunbiyi told her that the water in the river is sweet as honey and has healing properties from our mothers that came to this earth and also suffered deeply but never lost their shining star.

"Drink some of the water and keep remembering who you truly are," Ogunbiyi assured her. *"You are a one of a kind shining star that is on this earth for a reason. Never give up despite how hard things get."*

Tola saw tiny specks of light
floating on top of the water
as if someone had poured a giant
bucket of glitter. There was magic
in that river, it had a force that was
intangible but precise. As soon as
she drank the water, she felt all sorts
of emotions. But most of all, she felt
peace and happiness. She looked
at her reflection in the water and
saw a strong, pure hearted woman.
Suddenly, she looked up at the full
moon that sat high in the sky. She felt
happiness and tranquility surrounding
her.

"Thank you, for opening the door of my heart and SOUL. I am starting to understand who I am and the things I've never knew were possible before."

Ogunbiyi, lifted his arms and placed his hands on Tola's face and gave her a gentle kiss on her forehead. "I have to go now. My mission on earth is complete. You have a powerful tool now that will help you stand the struggles of the mundane world."

Tola didn't want him to go. *"What will I do without your guidance?"*

He spoke gently, his power simmering beneath his gentle exterior "I will always be with you. Remember, you are energy and energy transforms but never vanishes. You need to learn how to let go because we are all connected. It was meant to happen like this. Your transformation will lead to others transformation."

Ogunbiyi started fading away. Tola heard a gentle voice coming from the river that sang sweetly, *"He knows your soul. Everything else is just an ornament. You have understood who you truly are now, and as you reach within. Ogunbiyi will always be there inside of your heart and soul."*

When Tola heard that soothing voice, she was grateful to Ogunbiyi, El Caballero de Ifa, for his profound teachings. She placed her hands on top of her heart, closed her eyes and took a deep breath. Right away she felt the positive vibrations that Ogunbiyi had left inside her forever.

Something in her knew he was not gone forever. She knew he was out in the universe helping other shining stars remembering their true essence. Tola was able to sense Ogunbiyi's energy around her like a warm blanket covering her precious body.

Tola shouted, *"Thank you!"* to the incorporeal voice and continued to walk. The woman that had felt lost, not knowing where to go and having negative thoughts about herself and others, now felt much more empowered with her thoughts, words and actions that were meant to send vibrations that elevated herself, others and the world.

About the Author

Itzel Luna is a devoted mother of 2 girls, she loves to cook and try new vegetarian recipes. Itzel's journey took her to find her destiny. When she was in Nigeria she got initiated into Ifa and her spiritual journey began. She likes to write, meditate, is a practitioner of Raja Yoga, Iyanifa and with this book, a two-time author.

"This book is special to my heart because it's made from my inner work. Through memories, dreams, grief, meditation and death and life cycles. I believe that the soul choreographs one's biology and destiny, everyday we forget that the soul, our inner essence is who we truly are. We need to bring the awareness of the soul by constantly practicing that I, you, we, they are all the same golden stars, our only difference is our temporary body like clothes."

www.ingramcontent.com/pod-product-compliance
Lightning Source LLC
Chambersburg PA
CBHW060857270326

41934CB00003B/174